C000146151

'Sean Borodale is withou[t] [...]
new poet I have read sin[ce ...]
Journal raises the bar for us all and announces a
thrilling new voice in British poetry'
Carol Ann Duffy

'This book is a kind of uncut home-movie of bees.
I like its oddness and hurriedness, its way of catching
the world exactly as it happens in the split-second before
it sets into poetry. These are pre-poems, note-poems
dictated by phenomena. Their context is bees, but their
subject (intriguingly) is Time...'
Alice Oswald

'Borodale is an extremely accomplished poet... the most
beautiful expression of what it is like to live with bees
that you could hope to find'
Telegraph

'Sean Borodale's *Bee Journal* lifts the veil on the
apiarist's life and goes to the heart of the hive... The
dense and intense language is the verbal equivalent of
the honey that delights the tongue'
Sunday Telegraph

EX LIBRIS

VINTAGE CLASSICS

SEAN BORODALE

Sean Borodale works as a poet and artist, making scriptive and documentary poems written on location; this derives from his process of writing and walking for works such as *Notes for an Atlas* (Isinglass 2003) and *Walking to Paradise* (1999). *Bee Journal* is his first collection of poetry, written in Somerset where he keeps the bees.

SEAN BORODALE

Bee Journal

VINTAGE

5 7 9 10 8 6

Vintage
20 Vauxhall Bridge Road,
London SW1V 2SA

Vintage Classics is part of the Penguin Random House group of
companies whose addresses can be found at
global.penguinrandomhouse.com

Copyright © Sean Borodale 2012
Introduction copyright © Sean Borodale 2016

Sean Borodale has asserted his right to be identified as
the author of this Work in accordance with the Copyright,
Designs and Patents Act 1988

This edition reissued by Vintage in 2016
First published in Great Britain by Jonathan Cape in 2012

www.vintage-books.co.uk

A CIP catalogue record for this book is
available from the British Library

ISBN 9781784871130

Typeset in India by Thomson Digital Pvt Ltd, Noida, Delhi

Printed and bound by Clays Ltd, Elcograf S.p.A.

Penguin Random House is committed to a sustainable future for our
business, our readers and our planet. This book is made from Forest
Stewardship Council® certified paper.

for Jane, Orlando and Louis

Economists understand about work about as much as alchemists about gold.

Ivan Illich, 'Shadow Work'

INTRODUCTION

If you walk from the main road at Nettlebridge through the 'valley of the witches' west of the Roman Fosse Way, you would follow the black vein of the Upper Mells stream through decaying woods in which calciferous waters turn nettle roots to stone. You would enter the bee-fields of this book: a rough, lumpy meadow, a red ochred beehive in the 'L' of a blackthorn hedge. Here, the garden apples taste of vinegar and coal. A single pear tree stands close to the hive, old and lichenous; each April it blossoms and fruits. The pears, gorged on by magpies and wasps in the summer, will never ripen. In the early seventeenth century Michael Drayton's *Poly-Olbion* described the 'coal-flecked cheeks' of this valley's stream. In the year's dieback, with its wet, rotting hanks of cellulose, the place has what Lorca called *duende*: 'everything that springs out of energetic instinct . . . whatever has black sounds, has *duende*.'[1] This is the setting for *Bee Journal*, my two-year account of keeping bees. The location is peculiar; defining the honey and my language too. When the wider landscape parches in high summer, this shaded, humid locality divines its insects and flowers; re-builds itself delicately in colour, sugar, water and sunlight. Anyone who has looked up through the angles of its late afternoon will have experienced the sense of being underwater, in air thick with transparent wings. Celandine, dandelion, willow, primrose, cowslip, garlic, orchid, scabious, knapweed: the landscape's

---

[1] Gabrielle Garcia Lorca, 'The Duende: Theory and Divertissement' in *Poet in New York* (First Grove Press Edition 1955) 154.

ox-blood soils and river silts and crumbling clays are the earth from which pristine, nectar-bearing plants rise and flower, from which bees take their food.

In the early spring of 2009, I cleared a space for a hive at the end of the garden and drove up onto Exmoor to collect my first colony. Over the two years that followed, whilst making the usual checks and observations that beekeepers make, I wrote at the hive into a series of notebooks, the writing intrinsic to the process of beekeeping. These notes became *Bee Journal*. The sudden shift of scale, the intensifying air, these tiny creatures, the sheer mass of them, was electrifying. A different scale of thought; a different speed of time. Bees were my element, the hive was instrument and the landscape became a stage for these acts of writing. The range of the journal covers a 300-metre radius around the hive: the garden, the house, unmanaged woods, the edge of damp meadow along the stream, a main road. Writing on-site and in real-time stabilised fugitive details in the field of encounter. The journal, stained with wax, pollen, bee, was refuge to a record of erratic language in the uncertain process of its making.

Not so far from the factory fields of modern agriculture in North Somerset, in among the 'weeds' and seasonal destitution of the damp river valley, the bees I kept lived and declined. My notes and observations written among them accumulated as a counterspirit to everything I read about gaiacide: of nature as the site of crisis. Scrutiny of the immediate locale through the lives of the bees was my means of resistance. The pages that follow chart this over the circuits of the year.

I had two sets of notebooks: one set I took with me up to the hive and this became *Bee Journal*; the other set stayed in the kitchen, where I wrote as I cooked and prepared food. The notebooks of the hearth, which observe food in transformation, became *Human Work*. The landscape and lifetime of *Bee Journal* surrounds the landscape and lifetime of *Human Work*. Both books are located in their specific worlds of attention, but they also hold close proximity to each other. Sometimes a poem or a line makes a jump from *Bee Journal* into *Human Work*: the honeycomb in the kitchen of '7th August: Property' in *Bee Journal* is the honey that in *Human Work* fuels the dreams of the children in bed asleep in 'Toast and Honey'. The opening poems of *Human Work* make use of apples from the garden – the blossom of which was visited by the bees of *Bee Journal*. A line in the last poem of *Bee Journal* mentions Hestia, the Greek goddess of the hearth who shadows the domestic tasks of *Human Work*.

Radical geographies exist as the locality in which bees forage, fly, mate, swarm. Radical geographies exist in the production of human food too; in the unstated biographies of place and substance; in the global transport and transaction by which we bring food to the intimacy of our bodies. The metamorphosis that occurs in rendering substance fit to eat and in making food beautiful and lasting seems not so distant from the changes bees exert in turning nectar to honey: jars of preserve along a kitchen shelf; cells of honey within a comb. The complex of honey contains the trace of its provenance: the entry of 12th November 'Winter Honey' moves through the experience of tasting a granular, unpalatable honey harvested from ivy flowers.

I learnt to identify 'my' bees as distinct from those of other colonies; sometimes I found one stray, drinking from the edge of a small spring. The poem '26th July: In the Garden' is one such spacious moment of encounter; a point of nearness to the individual. At the hive, however, inside the increased effort of simultaneously writing and 'keeping' I experienced a pressure, a slight emergency of the senses. This raised my alertness to details of moment but also confounded the technical difficulty of writing itself. There is a truism in quantum physics that the world is always slightly, un-recoverably out of focus. My early attempts to sustain attention, to hold the nerve, inside the swarming noise and flight-paths of the opened hive were not always entirely successful (though I have only been stung three times). Poetic attention, in those obscured instants, filled in the gaps: a leap into chance. The lines of writing hold a course between intention to write into a moment and the magnetism of the erratic. Strange or distracting, those chance events cause a swerve into heightened experience or intense incomprehension. The concentration of the line wavers, like a strip of gold leaf inside an electroscope lifting and diverging from a metal plate in the presence of charge. Bees' eggs are no bigger than pinheads, a challenging scale for the human eye; the lack of focus in some of the entries is true to account.

Bee Journal represents another phase in a longer artistic project of mine to create a poetic form I call the 'lyrigraph', a word I coined from the Greek *lyric*, concerning the lyre, and *graphos*, writing. In the decade before I took up beekeeping, I had been making documentary poems about cattle markets and other urban-rural communities. I was writing whilst walking – texts for which the act of walking generated the metabolic rate or poetic pulse of the poem-in-progress. My book *Notes for an Atlas* contains thousands of encounters documented whilst walking a fifty-mile journey around London. I made (and screen-printed) texts which scripted the attempt to write about place, in situ or on location. I felt a need, in creating this term 'lyrigraph', to move away from the deadweight of making the poem appear *fait accompli* and into the moments when I felt most alive as a writer.

The lyrigraph, then, is a counter-poetics to the closure of a finished poem, in which the moment of writing is an intentional performance. The writing itself *is* the live performance. The text is its record; a transcript of live experience *of* the performance of writing. The performance of writing the lyrigraph is not the same as the latent performance in a playscript. Conversely, *Notes for an Atlas*, which is a primitive lyrigraph recording moments of possible 'poem' along its walk through London, became a live outdoor theatre event when Mark Rylance directed its performance as *Monument for a Witness*. Four actors worked in relay to represent the writer 'seeing' and 'hearing' the street, whilst 'walking' on a travelator set upon a plinth in front of the Festival Hall at Southbank. The piece ran live over eight nights at rush hour: relaying twenty-four hours of writing performed at an earlier time.

It is moments of such present, moments of such brief half-life on the scale of lyrical radiation, that vaporise into speech; and which the lyrigraph attempts to put down into writing there and then. The *potent present* is time dedicated to the making of such poetic utterance. I have tried to think of this time as specifically different to ordinary everyday time. It is *intended* time, for language on the brink of transformation. The *field theatre* of the lyrigraph is where such writing is staged; for instance, the radial landscape of the beehive. In *Bee Journal*, the phrasing and editing was carried out in real-time, in the chaos of the notebook, inside the acts of observing and writing. Sometimes I premeditated what I wanted to 'see' as I walked up to the hive. The journal grew between this mood of anticipation and what Bruno Latour has called 'the slight surprise of action'. I wrote while the image was still on the retina and the sounds hummed in the ear.

As you approach the hive, you enter the zone of its scent, a kind of aura: pine wood, honey, beeswax tinged with a slight mustiness. Even in the weak sunlight of a winter day, a few bees gather at the mouth of the hive on the sloped stage of its landing board. Peter Brook reduced theatre to this fundamental: 'I can take any empty space and call it a bare stage. A man walks across this empty space while someone else is watching him, and this is all that is needed for an act of theatre to be engaged.'[2] The figure I transformed into as I put on the costume of the beekeeper and approached the hive, notebook in hand, evoked in me the masked performer in a play. Well into the second year, I was feeling that the keeping of bees – an agricultural intervention – brings responsibility which cannot be squared against vicissitudes of ignorance. Whenever I was the beekeeper, I performed as the writer. My notebooks are stained with the life and death of bees, with the ink of my pen; from inside the continuum of their annual cycle: their noise, their scent, their flight. From time to time, late at night I would walk up to the hive and lean my head against the backboard of the brood chamber; listen in proximity to their sustaining noise in the darkness; the constellations of the Plough and Orion to the north and the south, night sky symbols of farming and hunting.

Unlike bumble bees, honeybees do not hibernate in winter but cluster around the queen generating heat through body motion. The noise I heard was a continuous signal stretched back over the fifty million years of their existence. The human lyric isn't entirely isolated inside the instant of its making. Lyric also stretches back over human vocal time; those who reinvigorate it, recycle it, use it to nourish or construct their own making of lyrical 'units', partake in that continuum. The energy of Homer powers the lyric units of Sophocles' tragic theatre; the energy of border ballads powers the *Lyrical Ballads* of Wordsworth and Coleridge. The fusion of domesticity and wildness of Dorothy Wordsworth's journals correlates with my own endeavour. This is the act of liberation as a reader, to divest a little of the energy of a text to alter the present.

In Henry Thoreau's *Walden*, his two-year account of living 'in the woods' and off the land, he warned that we are 'in danger

---

[2] Peter Brook, *The Empty Space*.

of forgetting the language which all things and events speak…
which alone is copious and standard'.[3] My own two-year project
was an attempt to write in a language patterned by the broad,
deep locality; to disturb my poetic tropes with the sensuous
texture of the bees. The German artist Joseph Beuys refers
to the 'rehabilitation of words' through new contexts; of the
need to transform language before it can *be* transformative.[4]
He made what he called *actions* in conjunction with specific
elements and *instruments* drawn from the circulation of everyday.
Beuys described elements as 'vehicles of experience… means of
rendering an idea visible.'[5] The 'actions' of Beuys as a performance
artist within gallery settings recall ancestral relationships with
meanings embodied in the material world. His use of a flashlight
is simultaneously a star setting over a grey hill and the light of
a hearth. This process of radical transformation through art can
carry alchemical weight. There were times at the beehive when
the writing enabled as well as disabled the process of phrasing.

The life of a beekeeper is a ritual life, as is the life of a writer.
Something like the instruments and elements of Beuys' actions
were also active in my performance of writing. Bees are by nature
(by our way of seeing their nature) physiologically and meta-
phorically alchemical. Instruments of my beekeeping included
the notebooks, a smoker, and the hive itself with its frames and
supers. Elements included language, honey, propolis, the bees and
the flowers. I light dry tinder inside the smoker. Once lit, I snap
the lid shut. It makes smoke when I move the bellows. There is
something potent to the flame of the match-light in conjunction
with the keeping of bees; a naked fire excessive and vital at once,

---

[3] Henry David Thoreau, *Walden* (Oxford World's Classics 1999; 2008) 102.

[4] Caroline Tisdall, *Joseph Beuys: Coyote* (Thames & Hudson 2008).

[5] *ibid.* 13.

acknowledgment of energy: the sugar in plants burning to carbon. The dry sticks made of stored sunlight I use to make smoke. There is the practice of rudimentary carpentry whilst making frames; the scent and feel of beeswax; the complexities of honey. All powerful elements among the ritually charged stations of beekeeping. There is the sustained, concentrated calm on opening a hive; both a violent intervention and respectful moment of wonder. Writing took place inside the polarities of these compounds and contradictions. The journal was an accumulative ritual process of repeated actions. The line of my walk between the house and the hive grew resonant; its physical wearing of a path, the visible evidence of purposefulness, reminded me of Richard Long's land art, *A Line Made by Walking*.

'You'll begin to understand the life of bees,' wrote the educationalist and philosopher Rudolf Steiner, 'once you're clear about the fact that the bee lives as if it were in an atmosphere pervaded thoroughly by love... Perhaps you noticed something about the entire nature of beekeeping, something, I would say, of the nature of an enigma.'[6] It's the enigma, ultimately, which motivates the investigation; the enigma of time within which work happens; it is the medium which links the geography of humans and bees. A cat's cradling of perception between two sets of consciousness. Within the first few days of the journal the bees explored beyond the 'proscenium' of their hive, they moved towards and eventually landed all over the house.

Slowly, the mirage of 'keeping' failed. I was present as a body fulfilling the interventional role of beekeeper. But what could I keep? I could keep a state of vulnerability. This was my sense: that as a keeper, I sometimes reached a corner or an edge at which the preoccupation with 'keeping' became one of futile anxiety. The

---

[6] Rudolph Steiner, *Bees: Lectures; with an afterword on the artistic alchemy of Joseph Beuys* (Gt. Barrington: Anthroposophic Press 1998).

poem '29th July: Interior' is a record of one such corner: fever-ishly, in the middle of the night, fearing the death of my colony, I circle back through Virgil's poem, the *Georgics*, to the corpse of an ox. Bugonia is the ancient art by which a colony of bees can be divined. An ox is killed without breaking its hide, its orifices are blocked; the corpse bricked up for a matter of weeks is opened at the auspicious time, releasing a new swarm. The bee produced was not a honeybee, however. Virgil's poem reminded me that losses in beekeeping are not new; that the means by which beekeepers sustain beekeeping can be precarious. Once, I walked into a swarm and was moved to trust the bees. I had them all over my hands, and took off my torn gloves to brush them into the hive. They didn't sting me. The sting is a part of the bees' integrity and vitality – it kills them to sting – and reminds us of our potential act of theft.

A thickness of time achieves different viscosities as we are re-tuned by the silence 'pixelated' by bees' flight. Seamus Heaney stresses the importance of the relationship 'between the almost physiological operations of a poet composing and the music of the finished poem'.[7] The deep time of the mineral air and the lyrical time of present experience coincide in the notebooks of *Bee Journal*. Honey holds information regarding the local environment; the thickness of honey is a readable part of environmental presence. Bees render our lives rich. Drones hang about in the hundreds throughout summer, eating the honey. For Rudolph Steiner, their role was connected to the wellbeing of the colony. Drones wait for the nuptial flight of a new queen; their large eyes serve to find her. But those large eyes, Steiner suggests, give the entire colony a greater vision, a greater intake of light through the community of their retina.

---

[7] Seamus Heaney, 'The Makings of a Music', *Preoccupations: Selected Prose 1968-1978* (Faber 1980) 61.

Beekeeping, like much farming, relates solitude to community, despair to camaraderie; urban or rural, there is always a network. To begin with I had the guidance of my friend Chris Lewis-Smith who worked with me in keeping the bees; a kind of Virgil-figure on my descent into the world of the hive and the darkness of apiculture. Bees live in the weather, subject to its minutia. In rain, the bees did not fly – some of my writing, too, was lost. The pages grew wet and soft. Sometimes I could not write or read what I'd written. This is the precariousness of the process and I wanted the performance to record such losses. The page is a perishable object, the field of a ruin, or of crisis.

'10th February: Queen' is one of the last entries in my hive notebooks and became the penultimate poem in *Bee Journal*. The coincidence of the date felt something like a superstitious experience, and for me the poem has become a homage to Sylvia Plath who took her own life on 11 February 1963. I wrote this *portrait* on an afternoon after we'd dismantled the empty hive. It felt odd to me that such an elusive, potent creature should become so disturbingly scrutinised, more than ever before, in death.

New life did eventually rise. As I write this now, bees live in the red ochred hive in the 'L' of the blackthorn hedge. And today, if you were to pass through this place, and stand under the weak afternoon sun with your feet sucked into the mud at the field gate, you would see bees taking flight from the mouth of the hive. Three years ago, two swarms turned up by chance: one took residence in a nearby ash tree in the black lightning mark that has since split, exposing the nest. The other swarm flew straight into the empty hive. In new notebooks, I have started to take a written impression of the air around them.

Sean Borodale, 23 January, 2016

BEE JOURNAL

I'd say it's toiling air, high up here;
steep with bees, and the beacon sun
burns
overlapping light, close to sundown.

Come to collect bees, our hive in parts.
Compound of fencing, stands of nucleus hives.
(Nuc,
new word.)

He just wears a veil, this farmer, no gloves
and lifts open a dribbly wax-clogged
blackwood box.
We in our whites mute with held breath.
Hello bees.
Drops four frames into our silence.

The air is like mica
ancient with thin flecks;
distance viewed through a filter of thousands.
I am observed.

Each box has the pulsar of its source. Porous with eyes
we wait in the spinning sun. The light is Medusa,
sugar of frayed threads; a mesh, a warp-field, all
the skin of our heads.

Forty miles west of here
a farmer was lifting, turning frames
in gloveless hands
from his box into ours.

Our hive now holds her bees,
night falls.

It sat behind us in the small red car;
noise inescapable.
Were we to crash it would be catastrophic.
Think! Do not think.

The noise of weight;
we carried this
through our proscenium of grasses
to the stand we'd built.

It is alive; unknown components we have:
small, small, small sounds composing one.

Untaped their door; two staggered out,
they fell
onto the landing board; first deaths.

Other broken bodies limped
not travel sick, but
ejected into a province of forget.

Please, no ill omen tonight.

Well-banded in our torchlight,
the bees all blackened to a clutch, a clot:
she must be there.
We stepped back in the air.
Petals, stamens, anthers of flower sex;
nectar will bribe these bees.

Lifted on thought I flew briefly. Human dance.

Gloves, gauzes, white suits slumped –
I live in here.
That strange squat Jack-in-the-Box
seems prominent – *out there*.

27TH MAY: GEOGRAPHY

Bees in the roof, bees on the walls
stitching the house in a net of flightways,
just like surveillance, just like snoopers
in the open air.

And they rig crack, lump, recess, ridge
to the commune of a memory;
and they rig it
to the thin low wide little door
of the North in the hive over there;

and they rig it
to our conversation and commentary,
and the brittle sweat's armada of frightened water
on our brows;

and they rig it, finally, to the minutes
of the sun's last floodlit bit of daylight.

I had to say, today, I said,
you have us locked inside your noise-truss.

You are a brain in impermanence,
coding, knowing, keeping
the latitude and longitude of this, our house;
each bee a synapse slowly forming an arrival.

And in your trance I had to say, this is
an afternoon of lifetimes tightened into knots.

You have gradated us:
vibrations, colours, trajectories of substance,
and the thermals
turning this house to align with yours.

The heavy brood frame
reeks with bees.
Still I have not seen
the queen's length, shape.

Amaze me, elusive maker of eggs,
your larvae catching light are lit
like life very young is lit
to see-through.

Your hive is a thought
all otherwise quiet;
a shape in a swaddling of noise
being sifted through;

each wing touch, leg rub, dance,
the air's big mass of flickers condensed.

Stop. *You, bee-friend,*
lifting a frame up to the light.
Sound of clicking, face peers close.
This is very sincere activity; we will be stung.

Various glow-blobs, dimmings of work,
living small bulbs of eye: note, bee glow.

29TH MAY: FEEDING SUGAR

I have the syrup feeder, its lidded reservoir
in both my hands,
going up to the hive for the third time ever.

Liquid I boiled and stirred the sugar into:
clear refined British beet.
It went, like magic does.

The plastic tub has an uncanny shifting weight.
I am their farmer.
I will for weeks give this, my gift.

30TH MAY: EXAMINING BROOD

Lifting the heavy brood frame weeping with bees
we are wax, translucent-feeling;
the weight already promises.

Being apiarists, we exploit this trust:
they let in our nerves.

They are impervious with process:
work-ethic tendency.
They do not pause
but play on in autoloop, and have phases.

We are in.

Jewellery box: I did not expect this strange calmness.
Eyes go steady with study of larvae,
womb, light, wax, bee eggs.

Still I have not seen the fountain of all,
where is *she*?
Must learn to find this instrument by heart.

One gold halo in a white room.

Neighbours-in-making, unlegged, unwinged.
No need for anything but mouth and anus now.
Will find flight.

This is a brain itself: congestion of language,
olfactory archive, register
of homeopathic light stored in amphorae.

You, bee man, lifting a frame to light, count only numbers.
You *are* human; what bees count must be more than parts.
Breathe on them your dream of honey-smeared taste.

They agitate and are in dream what sun pens.
Motherboard of many; each light, residual:
element, lumen, diode, valve.

This snapshot is vital; I take but cannot make.

I capture nothing – several drones are present.
Take note, they will be killed; should *I* take note?

5TH JUNE: BEE SMOKER

We went white-clothed from head to toe
with smoker:
Tin can with spout and bellow.

Smokery for bee visits,
each time hung up like fish or ham,
preserved.

They are transparent panes
when cut into;
their luminous glass flesh of times.

Few twigs and screws of paper
lit, smoke puffs and withers.

It makes a tenuous strange mark,
this mode of dissipation.

Note, if tapped the hive will roar;
did this; it did.
The battery test has worked,
some bumped the gauze.
Alive deranged edges of choked fire tapered.

This National hive is not a nation; its cedar box
was opened, saw their work like grains of rice.
My eye did not invent this?

Uncertain now, I must believe
I *did* count the tiny specks inside brood food.
Smoke veiled the scent of my amazement.

Brood food – I like that secret.
Secreted from the workers' heads
is royal jelly. That makes a queen.

Rain fell, smoke language drifted unsaid.
Will not use the smoke again, it seems unkind.

6TH JUNE: SUMMER NOTES

Today is anxiety.
No presence of the queen, maker of bodies.

Today is anxiety.
Not a length, not a gap between the working.

Today is anxiety.
Her own name frail as vapour just rubs off the tongue
wrong.

Who, if I call her,
who if I call in to the crawling tenements of workshop?
What should I call her? *New, central, unlit, a unit?*

Gauze, visor again, veil,
the white suit, until I, anonymous.

This is the beekeeper; generic, utility,
a slogan to be worn;
all-white billboard person on view.

Ochre-painted cedar, tiny boxed planet,
what else, what else?

Danger of mice, crawlies, varroa destructor
flattening a way through the streets of comb.

Must listen for
invaders.

9TH JUNE

All day they have dragged in
jewel-pins of nectar.

Now the whole of light rests.

Observe wet ground nettles have clogged with yellow roots,
flicker of water;
bee drinking,
knelt almost to lift from the trickle.

Nettles have grown into old men's bristles,
an endlessly rising Lazarus of bees.
This one bee is so newly built
it is almost impossible to give it time.

I watch its mechanism, its quartz pulse
drink bones of wetness from one of earth's holes.
Goes piloting up with added weight,
no doubt, its fuel-tank full.

Amazed at air's revolving energies. The sun:
each string of its hours is plucked and let slack.

14TH JUNE: SWARM?

What would you describe as commotion, friend
who watches from the window where the eyes
see the source of darkness,
and hear the shiver, fleck, and coiling twist,
a gutstring of bowed noise low down at home.

I did not quite expect that they would do this: go.

Examine,
almost crushing,
a thick slab of bees pouring out of the slot.

They went south . . .
False alarm. What next?

18TH JUNE: THE WORKS

Slow constant hum,
like a man will make when working
(or whistle).

Everything turning on duty in progression, as orderly;
touching and arcing points of weld.
Communication forms.

Long iron clouds,
because weather has importance, laws of conduct.
Stowing the world under rain
not yet heavy enough to fall.

The box is flooding with arrivals;
a weight measurable by thickenings of sound.

Experiment with this
in terms of how it's heard: up close, ear pressed
right to the jacket, shoulder-blade-thin panel back . . .

20TH JUNE: DUSTED
BEES WITH ICING SUGAR
(VARROA-PREVENTATIVE MEASURE)

With the hive tool prised the glued lid off;
slight cracking of propolis
(before I saw the citizens).
A sieve, a spoon; such words conjure baking.

This icing-sugar shower, this mad abrasive rev of wings
shaking the blizzard off with football stadium boos.
Grey ghost of bees,
of Pluto's.

Note, each bee grips with front legs
and flies the air across its thorax
on the spot.

13TH JULY

We checked. Bees have swarmed.

Nothing to say, except
we fed those left with syrup.

16TH JULY

The smaller bees are kittenish.
Tapped hive, the noise continues long.
Supposed to be a sign of health.
The drones are vast, bothersome.

12 Two thirds drawn comb on one side only.

1 Two sides drawn comb, a few cells filled.

3 Two sides drawn, 10% stores, queen cup broken open.

2 All drawn with 10% stores, no brood so far.

4 Drawn with some pollen, 10% stores, one empty
    queen cup, four bees feeding one bee with red tongues.

8 All drawn, some pollen, no brood.

5 All drawn, some pollen, no brood, surfeit of drones.

6 All drawn, some pollen, 10% stores, surfeit of drones.

7 30% drones, no stores, all drawn, one queen cup closed.

9 Not fully drawn, half to two thirds stores.

10 Drawn one side only, 10% stores.

11 Drawn one side, turned this around.

26TH JULY: IN THE GARDEN

I assume this creature is *my* bee.

There it is: one pulsing abdomen;
light brown, familiar, gently striped. Tongue
at drinking water.

Frail, how it concentrates
not solely for *itself*.
It makes one part.

What rhetoric the mind must be,
quite undisturbed.

Alas, how to read
mimesis;
not just reading what is ulterior,
ideal of a mother.

She needs water in this other mouth.
She
consists of minute projects,
like this alone.

How in her time
all co-exists,
not of itself.

And is she in?

Bees in irritated pieces;

touch is out of bounds.

               One head
put to the side of what is inside.

Be very quiet,
harvesters have made their place, a row of four.
Just details these, but seem significant;
all exactly as *I* found it.

Dewy limbs just under an eave of zinc;
the rain is a sound against the hive.

My ear listens to an inside side.

12   One side part drawn.

1   Both sides drawn, tiny proportion stores.

3   Both sides stores, no queen cup present.

2   Drawn, part stores.

4   Drawn, stores, no queen cup present.

5   Brood, capped and uncapped, white grubs. *Yes.*

6   Brood, capped and uncapped, white grubs. *Yes, Yes.*

7   Minute eggs, both sides. *Yes. Thanks.*

8   Drawn and stores.

9   Drawn and stores, some capped both sides.

10   Drawn and stores, both sides.

11   One side drawn only, turned.

First sign of new queen, mated and laying. *Alive.*

14TH AUGUST: BEE INSPECTOR

Today a DEFRA bee inspector clipped the wings of our queen.
What happened to those clippings?
Her flightless life is in that box of ours:
hoarded earth bit of her, no flight.

Nor will she collect her males into her mating flight
and fuck, and sever his genitals fiercely under the sun,
and creep back into darkness in that box again
she lays the eggs in for a lifetime's distance.

6TH SEPTEMBER: WILD
COMB NOTES

I have the surprise comb in September's hive:
topped between frames, great pale construction
occluded, skinned and nibbled clean
bear's-skull of paper-white wax.

I hold a knife
and cut at the block of crystalline honeyed brain.

I taste its juice; sweet gods of the evergreen
woods' taste;
crushed music, bars and epiphanies of dripping air;
aggregated cells
of each and every flower's oddness there;

this sugar-map.

My tongue swarms like a fire has been lit
clean of its obstacles.
Right on its wet hearth-slab: solar heat.

I think, each bee's six heels
may be callipers for cell's wall angles.

12TH NOVEMBER: WINTER HONEY

To be honest, this is dark stuff; mud, tang
of bitter battery-tasting honey. The woods are in it.

Rot, decayed conglomerates, old garlic leaf, tongue
wretched
by dead tastes, stubborn crystal, like rock. Ingredients:

ivy, sweat, testosterone, the blood of mites. Something
human
in this flavour surely.

Has all the clamber, twist and grip
of light-starved roots, and beetle borehole dust.

Deciduous flare of dead leaf,
bright lights leached out like gypsum almost, alabaster
ghost.

Do not think this unkind, the effect is slow
and salty in the mouth. A body's widow in her dying year.

It is bleak with taste and like meat, gamey.

This is the offal of the flowers' nectar.
The sleep of ancient insects runs on this.

Giant's Causeway hexagons we smeared on buttered toast
or just the pellets gouged straight from wax to mouth.

Try this addiction:
compounds of starched cold, lichen-grey light. What else seeps
out?

Much work, one bee, ten thousand flowers a day
to make three teaspoons-worth of this
    disconcerting
    solid broth
of forest flora full of fox. Immune to wood shade now.

Listen to the rain, the rain, the rain, like the wings and legs of bees walking across bees, like the lyre of a thought, a whole possible instrument of insects.

Listen to the rain, more rain, treadling earth to the sodden cold wet spun heads of this room, pacing the winter to and fro . . .

13TH DECEMBER: EVIDENCE OF COLD SNAP, A PAGE OF SCATTERED BEES FROM THE HIVE FLOOR

I torchlight through carrion;
the wooden effigy, cold-blood, crutch of one.

Here on this page, dour with weeks of stamped cold,
lie some twenty specimens.

Sodden in commune, grey with mould,
collapsed over hoops, distended structures.

A crouched patch of gut,
a crippled fur, crimped leg, ragged wing.

How to reactivate this mess?
No farmer could do it.

18TH DECEMBER

A transformer buzzes in the box, is tumbling on its core,
like winding the dark slowly over,
biding what it is, just conscious where-
abouts, a who? Without being there.

MIDWINTER

No bees venture.
Just one day's quiet after another's.

7TH JANUARY

Four inches of snow. The hive a hut
of silence and darkness.
I found a stick and scratched
a small translucent tunnel to the door.
Are you in there?
I've brought some light and air. No answer.

19TH JANUARY

Everything is senile.
I ask
   the box to
speak
   about
its bees.

14TH FEBRUARY: SONG

This beekeeper is bleak with lack
but he can heave a hunch up on his back;
he still can lift what needs begin a year,
and go out white from head to toe in gear,
under the blackbird's stark evocative
and murderous motor of keeping active,
since the hive is magnetic and grows magnetic . . .

Morning has streams of river sun,
cold stamping cold.

The bees are not out. Listen
to the grey rut of world,
the frozen track steams.

The bees are not out, listen.
I walked up close to the body of bees.

Just a door from this into their unlit state . . .
my mind sketches a congested bulk
in the cavity of the boards.

You have a manmade hut.
Do not shrug and go gloomy,
do not tip down your ball of
glued body parts.
The trick is life.

The bees are not out I muttered aloud.
But I just had my hands
rubbing their sticks of papery fingers,
I just had the nagging aeons, the quicksilver touch
of exposure getting me to keep still
to take its utter quiet of a picture.

The whole of the north is turning its screw into shatter.
The winter winds out.
How slow the Plough-memory of night dips and turns.

The bees are crouched in the door.
Quiet, I said, *listen*, I said.

They fan out of the door a Minerva beard,
lay out the flight paths, the locks of hair,
combing the air's amnesia to a noise.

Do I dare to trust . . . these pets? They are not that.
Now as the rain skims down through rattled air
the last dead things, like skeletons of stones,
catch on my feet: *bee-friend*, the late dead things,
the skeleton of Christmas, fireworks of midnights vaporised,
the awkward purposeless haste of visitors . . .
These bees are visitors, how long they last, our guess.
The skeleton of song, the robin's cry note entering the bees.
Time very arthritic; the clock's joints ache.
Black bees, like models made of tar and grit, get stuck.
The queen inside them all; they, wall and bedding, cluster
walls' eyes, measuring and smelling, fitting . . .

1ST MARCH

Catkins.

7TH MARCH

Snowdrops.

12TH MARCH

The hive I opened today, bee friend, the comb empty.
Green lumps of mould strewn, the floor;
clogged dead understorey.

Morgue house it seems,
bees in their hundreds doomed out of time.

Some are just still living, operative. Are they in this or do
they mechanise just fractions of the consequence of living.

Autopsy, the worst atrocity of winter spell
has . . . under charge . . . famished guts,
a rotted lump of wreck.

Is your mind *dwindling*?
A conscious collective losing thought . . .
I thought, not you again.
New space for more to bring the sun in on the mouth.

Don't speak, it might use up presence. Why so weak?
What song is this which kills you singers as you sing it?
The cold is serious.

This is
our crematorium of hexagons, wild with crumbling debris;
crumbling
not so burnt as burnt-out, building *of* broken rooms.

Blown vaults, picked at with lean hands
gaunt from expenditure; creaky ticky bees

ransacked the last unforthcoming . . . opened cells:
Ivy honey too rock hard crystalline to extract.

(Advice: spray combs with water.)

What are the ends of winter-bees like then?
Brittle suitcases of fleeting trickery, empty.
I closed your box . . . Good luck.

9TH APRIL

General unburdening of wings, exclaims existence.
Our bees are not yet lit but stagger out
like gauze mantles for a gas light.

Pear tree changed to expressive.
Soon to explode crook-ends
from its thousand chins, knuckles, kneecaps, lids.

Touch: firm sprung leaf,
new horns of cattle, unpacking flower.
Touch: a crane yard of construction.
Almost seemed it would never happen.
I said almost seemed . . .

Now this roaring of boom-time, this action:
just a slip of the ancient.
The celandine remembers sun-winched paraphernalia.

You fly over.
You fly through . . . to the *other*.

(Right now an iron fleck creature
plays havoc with my writing hand;
it does not walk my trail of ink.

Observe the quivering body, legs scarce,
the head's pinprick.
This is I, it writes
in meandering sketch.

I blow it away
to a scrofulous bud . . .
glistening.)

The air sings white edges, *parts* of lichens . . .

20TH APRIL

Frost, and frost yesterday
and last night.

Strong little moon picked at your bones.

The pear on the brink
of unpacking its blossom.

One-bee marquees,
nectar festivities, tents.

One-day-only stalls of druggy sugars,
the beers of flowers.

Everything is dragged awake;
puts on its music clothes.

2ND MAY

The North Wind leans against your house
containing a mind of its own again;
its song, its bursts of breath are wilful cold reminders
of the dangerous airs.

Slowly you are tuning yourselves
into the small misheard scales, into a purpose.

A bee, a tine being struck was out:
sound like a rooting of thin flash
in liquid form poured from a bucket the size of an adult
tooth.
Magnet of listening, I to hear it
turned the pole of my head.

The hive door is there,
the landing board's grey slope of bleached wood.

One worker there,
banded as piano wire, freakish hands strumming.

Those *are* wings.
I was out, all my apertures very unfrightened.
Calm holes in my head heard the exact creak
of breaking nettles across the buzz.

Silence please!

Glass air, glass furnace hit with a hammer. Sun
wildly lighting. Who is that smashing the walls?

If I extracted myself from the game
of being a keeper of danger,
the silent white suit which I wear
would unstuff itself, and hang
from the peg by the back door forever.

I would go naked, raw-boned, into that garden
if I extracted myself from this game of being keeper of bees.

I would go like a gaseous glass flesh
with a glassblower's mind
expanding over the very idea of my empty space.

1ST JUNE: HUM

Yesterday their tower-block of discrete units
was making new language out of cross-lapsed phrase.

No cease;
this madness is perpetual.
All works to a story fanning wildly
flames of plot outside the little door.

They must maintain the level of internal heat
to keep alive the characters they are.

Grip on and buzz;
emanation in the mad still air.
I am caused quietly
to hear.

These spy ears clamp
noise slowly gaining me
a radar bleep
in its circumference.

Looped with winding,
the armature of a motor, drifts of hum,
tone warp –
my mental notes cannot unknot.

Put seven frames into the Honey Super,
having taken the empty syrup feeder.

Unwearying winding of light high noise;

bees batting this pen and poem's paper.
Bee on my gloved hand,
heads of bees brushing over.

Small irritated power-tool shape of sound;

a spark of music, a score
going right down through my head;
a sheet of music
grinding the halves of my brain apart.

I am two beekeepers, just in phase:
two suns, two fields of air,
two lapsing horizons, superimposed.

5TH JULY: BUSINESS OF FRAMES

The hive needs frames
or brace comb fills the space.
So I make frames: I learn the work
of making batches up from pre-fab kits.

My concentration collects to beekeeper dew-point
demanding the kitchen, all of its table.

Knock tenon to mortice,
Who's there?
The foundation, a sheet of stamped-out coda.

Note, each mutating shadow of a tack
creeps to its nailhead . . .

. . . 12 frames are stacked.

6TH JULY: BRACE COMB

Part of the moon bees have
was found in flowers:

the unseen stance, the quality of things
in human palm-sized pieces;

a vital organ of two days' deep work
growing a topography of common;
the wicks of eggs,
new and clipped.

I twist the brace comb off
and brush the bodies
of bees alone;
legs hooked in their world hang.

The rusks of hexagon
are mute strength in volume;

plain as a Shaker would fashion a drawer;
materially earnest,
divine, pure of toil.

Agitated,
you opened the hive under a great parasol
to keep the hive rain-free;
shaking of workers into air.

And there were the frames,
fat wads of untasted honey
now and *here*: animal, particular weight.

Bees, tail-raised scorpions of moment.
Scores of drones,
the heart of drone time.
Beware: increasing roar.

Stabbed!

Three stings to the right hand.
You, one to the neck.

Witches of black poison went screeching
figures of eight,
all broomstick and flight path.

Black poison throbbed.
My rivers wretched, staggering at undertow,
gripped my feet.

And you, agitated, no sight of the queen,
whispered, as if in a calm state, *Are you there?*

Two queen cups, stored, like closed kegs of brew.

17TH JULY: KILLING DRONES

Today cut comb with drone cells from the lower frame.
Too many drones,
one tenth of all here this month;
they eat the stores.

Capped brood in ancient pots.
(Suspect no queen present,
she with clipped wings, gone.)
Respect the unborn dead.

Hatched heads waggle, *they* are trapped;
they understand
the pageant of the mating flight will come.
And yet not born yet, these fated.

Two queen cells ripen fat with burden;
evolve same plan.
(Winding sound increased.)
Which queen will wake first?

This game we hold and do not possess but use.
This farm is cities;
good health;
wing sheen like threshold stones.

Kneel eyes;
note, no graffiti of foul brood or mould;
comb dark with capped brood *is* pixels.
Wings good, not ragged; the honey clear,
will not take yet.

Took one board of comb with hatching drones;
heads chewing out their caps.
Threw the buoyant, tarry, dark wax into the river.
Barge of ballast: heads a trout may seize.
Slow flows, away it goes,
twelve-headed river-hearse of the emergent.

No flame for them.

23RD JULY: NOISE & WASTE

Today the hive
is trying out *its* harmonics,

a weepy low fugue I think to burning sun.
The loss of flowers is overwhelming:

dry sheaths and packets
stapled onto brown skulls.

The nagging air swings gibbets of drought.
Some clumps of the world are barred.
The dump stinks in flowerbeds, weedbeds,
and the river's clogged two miles of hemlock rots.

Mangled carapaces fall out of air
skinny in their little traps of make-up.

A chimera of scrap parts.
Grass-blade emerald twisted.
Glitter paste of bumps & grazes.
The air's ears are traumatised,

and on the flames of the hour
just a whiff of decline,
just a whiff more.

The white dry heat jangles;
it's like a kiln is shaking at the corners.

Tomorrow,
must search the dawn's damp ash
for broken mirrors.

29TH JULY: LATE AFTERNOON

Bees in other hives out there are dying in droves.

Now,
now,
and now,

the wind drags bleakly, other horizons paw
at our premise, edge, dregs of far points,

anemophilous noise
which shifts and lifts a tambourine
of black, black news.

Tree-flapping, guitar-like,
string-scrape signatures;
the wind's bee chanting scores,
potential, potential collapses.

This is an uncertain, uncertain tragic time of *ours*:
Rocks in the field, like *old* stone hives.

29TH JULY: INTERIOR

My bed here, say four hundred yards south-east of the hive,
my bed here.

Awake in the zoo-dead-of-night
I listen in on the cages of the day's hours.

There is that question,
trapped and circling a hole in the floor.
A slurry of collapsed swarm agitates in there,

like the very black bowl of a
dead stare into itching solid.

And there in that bludgeoned hole is the idea of a calf,
not broken, but fully bruised, and blocked up with clay plugs.

Mistaken bees blackly weep from its ears.

The colony has one time: it's like a gas
dispersing towards the lowest of pressures.

7TH AUGUST: PROPERTY

A frame of honeycomb is in the kitchen:
just a candle, vigil, out of respect.
It's like a body I visit
laid on the table's midnight.

The smell is first; under its pinewood resin
the smell of light is in a miracle:
I – criminal – touch

its tear-easy skin of skeletal reef.
(Best use of space for minimal effort.)
No waste for them, just work,
and days of nectar flow are nearing end.

Flowers are here, springs of them,
wells and weightless drops of briefest sex;
a wax shroud turned down at its corners;
a dead skin most beautifully scented,
drawn out of dark.

When touched,
observe the way
that light swells in the crack
and golden-eyes.

But it is cold,
I paid for it with hooks across my flesh.

25TH AUGUST: AFTERMATH

columbine   pea   dead nettle

foxglove   tansy   hemp agrimony

  herb Robert   Sedum

                               Welsh poppy

meadowsweet   St John's wort
                     thistle

27TH AUGUST

The spider's season opens,
rat tooth-marks begin to appear;

almost just a tempering of vision.

So in a coat
I go up to the ochre house of you in there.

How bees touch and re-align their touch.

Light in migration;
noise of a body in continual repair . . .

29TH SEPTEMBER

Archangel sunlight
held to a flower's remnant,
a weighing of balance in the sway of asters
I saw two days before,

as though the angled plane
of the flat face of September's sun
had made each flower's inflorescence
mirror its gift.

We are inflected:
note, bees give by this.

7TH OCTOBER: WASPS

Torrents of wasp – five at once, fifty, erratic, persistent.
Bee peace is bombed at this house, but
distortion in their world *is* articulate.

The air's single cell is clear as a bauble, and delicate.
They know the invertebrate bubble of the planet's life-jacket
and do sustain it – this weird filigree of livid minute.

It seems mirage to us, sceptical ill-tuned folk;
bees heatwave off the hive's wooden mouth.

As for wasps, it's like
short sparks which jump from loose plug leads
into an engine's block.

Today then, I watched a threading of loose ends.

11TH OCTOBER: MICHAELMAS DAISIES

Bright day, afternoon, no precise time,
the hour-light at sunlight's maximum.
Michaelmas daisies are set to now.

Alight honey bee, I do feel
the extremity of your spectrum
that homes on an unsteady cymbal of flower's radial.
I heard it shivering tissh as you touched on its platform;
a close-up protracting of tongue suck in a zip-noise;
a faint sweet wet from a nectary's spring.

We observe the yellowness of dying leaves:
it's like gates, it's like precincts being drawn
to 3D's infinity point of perspective.

The shawl-work of summer has grown unwoven, tuned into
a brittle, rottable music of roughage and stubborn dregs.

The earth-she wanders, going blind and odd,
like air, pushing a trolley full of dead flowers;

is that not you, Persephone, or Eurydice, or just a likeness
creeping?

Listen,
small pitch patch of bee-wing song
is strung with a sound made of now's last flowerheads.

Maybe just
our time ticks because we have a time to accord to;
and all the machinery is lifted by briefest experience.

Echoes are something more quiet
than a world's bee paused on a ledge at an edge
for a life of a few weeks
cycling up from millennia's blackness.

(*We are played in your existence;*
the Shadows we bring
fall just a note's breadth
off your heart-rate's strumming.)

16TH OCTOBER: SUPER CHECK

Removed the Honey Super.
No stores,
just a dry, papery wax-comb of empties.
No sugar syrup touched;
what is wrong with supplements?

Stand mesmerised
at this landing board.
It is familiar, all-relevant –
a collateral winding of wire-string song.

Think what paths would be
if *we* could envisage
flights tracked to their nectaries'
pin-point co-ordinates.

A round dance tells trails
in mid-air's mile or so round-trip.

We bring, bee friend, yellow pollen on our legs.

In human terms, it seems OK.
Your bright sharp blackthorn-rickety bodies pass each way.

I lay a minute's judgement:
minute, small, perhaps a touch vacant,
a field-slack lethargy, something I dreamt
still nameless, coagulating its weak-spot under our nose.

Burdock burrs gather and catch on our gauze
as we hack

the thicket clear of the hive
for winter air to not stagnate.

We suffer damp, dear neighbour – you should not.

Today, lifted the hive's in-winding with our gloved hands,
set up microphones to amplify, and catch
and keep and zoom in on your snatch
of fieldsound din;
what makes your orchestration, dialect, anima: in.

You are studding our vestments.

Tonight,
I transcribed each track to a score,
a foley for winter-prayer to repeat
a river wound onto spools of tape-like time
like bolts of fallen light you whisper in sine-
wave. And I play back
to will alive your hyper-thyroid slurred to human slack.

At queen's depth,
you were fast-forwarding a stress;
this is your speed of conversation;
just a fizzing spaghetti-
junction of swerves
over your sanctuary's inner sanctum.

How privileged we are to lower ears in
and slow to one wingbeat-per-second,
go between headphones into deep stereo.

I have your hive's unique vertigo

at 24 bit, 48 mega hertz,
digital, precise, approximate.

20TH OCTOBER: BROOD NEST HONEY

Black honey in its dark brood cells
is a wild liquor of ecstatic work.
Bright sun and gauze exhaust its details.

We fall to our second winter, bees.
The grass flaked out of frost white bones last night,
emaciatingly bright.

Your ultra-commune is still unlocked, you fly,
but feel the globe of cluster remembered
like vapour ghost breath smoke-ring trick of circular,
contracted.

And we, beekeepers,
can only open the book part way to read what is unsaid.
Not being your drones we do not see like you.

Eyes fed and lit up.
Eyes starved and kicked out.
That was a drone's life, all summer's sight.

We lean on our human eyes,
absorbed into honey black with cocoon stain.

28TH NOVEMBER: MUMMIFIED
FLOWERS

Day-of-the-dead twenty-six days late.
Black star of cow parsley is fate
in cellulose; black hand bone of meadowsweet
a fountain's ruin; and underground, live root and antiseptic.

We dead-of-insects keep one crane fly in the house,
dead family ghost invertebrate –
I learn to love its structures.

In your bee-garden, tethers slacken;
it is all ribs and crucifixion-
styled event
in slippery brown black;
the black of winter trout,
for example, leaps to mind.

But it is plants whose flower you sucked I study:
now pharaohs bound in corpses of stiff earth;
their embalming is theirs.
Frog faces made vague of body.
St John's wort stands unzipping one side.
Yarrow, charred twig in dry mouth.

I could go on in this crypt voice;
the vault is a museum for muses.

I look over flower-beds, catacombs, tilted spear leaf,
amphorae of dusts.

One preserved canoe oar's decrepit end
of what a flower needed to get over;
sandal-made footprints of remain,
frozen effigy of airs.

The biology is lessons in death.

I snap a pipe of hemp agrimony off.
Its ice is un-scrolled papyrus,
a very old hieroglyph for 'dead light'.

Two black leg-stumps stick up where the earth
walked a plant up. I swear
it was there
carrying a gourd of honey in its hair.

Checked hive,
removed base-board at noon,
hoping to dry
the damp air soon.

Fiddled out dead wings
from the mesh,
journal of a bee's head,
particular bits

of a knee fell down,
sting, tongue,
dropped from the grille,
but these dead bees are insulation.

Looked to the south:
a moist flood-lamp heaviness of sun's
frost shape.

The hive black with damp,
bogged in burial, mouldy bedding.

It's hunger you grow,
keeping a queen light in your dream sight.
She at the tip of the pyramid of your hierarchy
but it's different.

Outside, broadly, gingerbread dusklight;
a granular snowfall litters woods.

I slide the board back in, close you up.

16TH DECEMBER: VARROA
DESTRUCTOR

We haunt our bees with tiny regular checks.
The board below the hive exhibits mites,
it is quite clear
a change has altered us and arrangements.

The parasitic present is in chains.
Home: sudden prison.

Black as grit stare of particulate;
moody revealing of a plague;
destructive, irreversibly inlaid
into this cedar-box of drag.

Pinholes in the day's air, the plummet breathless:
I wheel still, bend my gauzed eyes,
blind in the mystery
of its onboard navigator, assessing parasite.

Appendages:
those mites make apertures and drink out bee,
the hole stays open for this beverage:
copper blood.

I have rehearsed the snag.
Now it is real weight, life's ferment, quiet it is.

The mite-count reveals eighteen:
crab-legged, as described in books,
flat button-shell.
I grow words I would spit:
oxide black, vitreous as slag.

Day biting, and the North's trees hiss,
and the North's wind's catastrophic noise
is stiff toes tripping over stones of a problem.

Curse
the arched cloud-fretted sky
that brought this, blows with sickness.

Rush to the house, and make enquiries.
The whole indoors is bent with disaster.
Phone down: I've sent for medicine.

18TH DECEMBER: SNOW AND INTERVENTION

Unscrew the cap, invert and squeeze
this bottle between frames into bee-gap.

(Water, saccharose, citric, oxalic, formic acids
& propolis extract,
diverse, unspecified, essential oils of what?)

A stagger of waiting
leans over the hour's clock-hand's seconds.
Jutting harp strings of light,
ligaments of noise take flight.

It's like a head being tapped out:
the weaker bees mass and fan at the door's ledge,
become a gangplank of intent to leave.
They slow-wing to the snow-floor.

The blackbirds are interested,
landing an assembly to constrict this unfortunate rink.

For an hour of daylight
the hive clears out the bric-a-brac of infested.

Before I go, I smear thin belts of their own honey back
along brood-frame bars.
Hangs of it plumb into the dark.

How did it go, this song of chemistry?
It's like a dream it should not be so,
bees misjudging the gaunt-of-heat world.

A hundred bees dead at a touch – that is not much
of thousands in a box,
but, black on the snow they go,
dropped bag of dead luck.

We do observe your plight – We, and the blackbird
in our danger. Observe – merely, yes.

21ST DECEMBER: SOLSTICE FOR BEES

The sun leans at its annual alignment:
bare day and short,
the sky bleached and chattering with a slight adjustment.

Light's skeleton puts back its fingers and flicks
the spectral end constant,
and bees just switch the wires of their song opposite;
winding the same sound the other way up.

Like hanks of yarn, this endurance of eavesdrop
grows wound and looped, and invariably it twists
between the wings and the ear.

May you come back
through the hole in the world's syllable.

I do not take the honey but lift it down:
the jar of it on the high shelf
is a ghost of goings-on,
a kept world-part of their summer,
and having it is prying on wood hedge, forest floor.

I have the whole life coat of light passed through it,
hanging by the tail over the table edge.
It is smeared with flame.
I have to drag up flame by the face
and cradle it like candlelight,
and it stares me out of my wits in this gloomy
month's crisis.
You, honey, pervade this place.
Its gatherers are on ritual guard through rites of famine.
Poverty becomes bones,
bones fingers, fingers loose, and loose the showman
on the stage of its miracle –
I cannot forget that word's
attempting arc over all silence.
Miracle, another word for this,
opens gold gates: a paraphrase for survival.

5TH JANUARY: IN THE GARDEN

Off-key is a slow angel of returning cellulose;
its sugars breed blindly underground.
All of snowlight's heartbroken month is scratchy
and cut back to a diagram for pruning.

Requirement: for the legacy to work.
Requirement: for the wild tendency
of light to return on its wheel of the nights
the bare sun;

       out of its ephitaphion
to call up the signature ghosts of green limb.

It is lavish with cold, it is almost insane.
Bees, in your wax insulation,
some of you sleep the raw, leftover, virtuoso
of you all; it diminishes daily.

6TH JANUARY: EPIPHANY

Each day's length's procession is hummed barefoot.
Like martyrs, some roll the road's infinity over frosty thorns.

May you carry your mother-queen to the year's haven,
at 1500 eggs-per-day speed.

13TH JANUARY: FALSE SPRING

Week's long hoax of mild weather
and bees wander like fools.

Up in the woods' hedge, catkins are no hope,
not yet let down smeared with yellow.

And only points of shoots are protracted – hand against hand,
finger to finger – and no crocus flower's first food, no protein.

Beekeepers are despairing on the telephone,
dream of cloches on the springtime floor.

Helios is given bonfires by some.

15TH JANUARY: HERB TEA

I read of a herb tea for bees
in which nettle, chamomile act as the basis.
It fortifies the problem of keeping bees,
but that is the problem: keeping.

I read of exchanges,
i.e. a formic acid in the nettle.

Bees bring this trace
and net it through the wild we call our garden,
as they work it.
Formic acid for nectar, pollination: this is trade.

I go to the sanctuary kitchen to make the tea,
add grains of salt and their own honey (10%) to boiling water.
(Be warned: imported honeys most likely
contain the nosema or foul brood spores.)

It cools to stone-heat on the side.

Liquor to set on the crown-board of the box
now winding steam abracadabras, plant oils
wetted to aroma;
the steel saucepan turned ancient.

And then, like a car mechanic, opened and closed the hive's
bonnet,
turned back over the chewy clay in deep footfall without the
brew.

24TH/25TH JANUARY: BEES DIE

29TH JANUARY: APOLLO MOUSE

Suddenly the house is dishevelled;
all in the sixth sense way of things,
a gaunt, empty, weight of bereavement.

A tramp mouse moves in; we know by excrement:
an Apollo from cold stone and bitter hunger.

Still, it is the coldest winter on record.
So much has changed in the way of house-keeping:
wax bitten shreds of body and furniture.

A dust-coating thickens to a taste's spectre,
and the quiet lack of bees is weighty.

The quartz honey upstairs is tampered loose.
You could not eat what was painstakingly gathered.

But it's like a hearthstone, a house,
for earwig and weather finding its door open.
Three days and squatters are regular,
infest the house; each as vagrant as any dweller.

Your trace is treasure,
despite the house mouse and dirt.

2ND FEBRUARY: PROOF

I go to the shelf where the honey lives,
and say, this is testament: bees did exist.

10TH FEBRUARY: DISMANTLING
THE COMB

Morning drizzle at ten a.m.
We open the hive, bee friend, last time
& it's like entering Pompeii,
much like that gritty, accumulating, reduction
in voice you get in shock;
for a minute we just hang up our arms
with frames of comb and stop.

Look, they are just where they were.
I did not expect to see a bee's point of death
like a chink in a protractor's half circumference;
sky perfect on wings, a storm-paddle sun like a torch left on
in a dead woman's hand.

We lift comb after comb only to find segments
of the cluster,
a sliced globe of clinked and magnetic sister.
And the queen, there:

intermission.

The room's sarcophagus of waft
ripe with not-quite embalmed must and antiseptic strange resin
staining our lungs and skin,
frames of beekeeper's mind.

There's an illness and beauty of detritus.
Our hands touch to face, finger, lip;
tongue takes smears of the gagging, like pollen of taste.

A slow word racks between our ears, once,
to conclude the problem: 'Dead'.

I run back for bin bags to take off the comb,
to burn the brood nest, to bag and to burn.

Keep two frames, friend, to observe, choose, loosen, lift
the very centre of the cluster right here
onto the kitchen table, under the light.

I rub one finger across stopped bees.
They in their cells headfirst, did they just stop there?
Soft as iron filings, grown lifted, quilted
with magnet.

A troubling soft streak –
they should rise and attack, but no instinct,
no quirk of uprising, only lack of resistance.

Our day has shrunk to the atrocity: brood-nest's
black pots, empty shops, eye sockets, pockets,
the perfected model of a fatal act.

Something else will re-invent it –
moths, mice, lice will eat it.

I torch into cells – eyes fit and focus-pull
in descent – to the fairytale's well.
It's like the grain of a moon, a spoon-back of pale no one,
just the pail of an egg's dry opal empty of hunger.

Every pit has a rice grain in it.
This is our prognosis: starved house.
She was laying in a warm spell, she was deluded
by a freak of the mild, unreal spring,

hazels just days off manufacturing
their dreadlocks of pollen;
how close she was, how close.

Stare, friend, an end, bees still in cells,
preserved shut-winged, fluttering by breath – that's death,
like stuck in strobelight.

Crusty oxide: describe the sealing cap
part-chewed like a split boil,
the white wet wax sheen of a grub not yet shrunken.
On the threads of our apiarist's eyes
we dangle into the nursery, count, re-count
roughly forty new eggs, died dividing their cells.

We house in our hands the corpse of a city:
cell-ends, dog-ends,
smells of apple, Germolene, urea.
We bag up thousands: foresters, workers,
dismal in drizzle.

I keep the queen, she is long in my hand,
her legs slightly pliant;
folded, dropped down, wings flat
that flew her mating flight
to the sun and back, full of spermatozoa, dronesong.
She was made mechanically ecstatic.
I magnify what she is, magnify her skews and centres.
How downy she is, fur like a fox's greyness, like a thistle's mane.
Wings perfect, abdomen subtle in shades of brittle;
her rear legs are big in the lens;
feet like hung anchors are hooks for staying on cell-rims.
Veins in her wings are a rootwork of rivers,
all echo and interlace. This is her face, compound eye.
I look at the slope of her head, the mouth's proboscis;
her thin tongue piercing is pink as cut flesh, flash glass.
Some hairs feather and split below the head.
Those eyes are like castanets, cast nets;
woman all feral and ironwork, I slip
under the framework, into the subtle.
The wing is jointed at the black leather shoulder.
I wear it, I am soft to stroke, the lower blade fans.
Third generation queen of our stock,
you fall as I turn. I hold your hunchback;
a carcase of lightness, no grief, part animal, part flower.

3RD JULY: GIFT

A noise is on the loose, today;
black winding pendulum weight of core
by the main road to Radstock.
I take a saw to cut down the bough of a swarm.

The air's innards have sprung apart.
I am netted in trawls of strumming bee.
Can I say
what kind of halo absorbs me?

In and in and in a morass, fast place, race,
roadside and twenty years of brittle bramble
thick with bees,
thorns snagging my beekeeper's costume.

I did not expect a calm lack of resistance like this.
Not one sting as I handle fizzing thousands,

entering the physiology of a heatwave;
their aspect, divine as electrons;
physically deranged sound
like a fool holding its freedom.

You *are* winged strange kind, you are nerval.
Inside your fluency,
mirrors facing all mirrors shade back to eternity.

Standing in the middle of your intellect:
must catch and keep.
My shroud conceals a skeleton of tensions, not me; I'm right out
in the open livid whirlwind of metropolis rid of its rooms.

I bring this hive,
Come in.
Bees from hands drop slowly as honey.
I close the lid on them, I wish the willing in.

Bring in a sound like Hestia, like hearth, like heart.

And they convey
the queen flame through the door.
I'd swear
you are descendants of the dead that swarmed last year
from here;
the width of your banding, that particular
taper of abdomen, colour . . .

I leave the box to gain its anima.

Now, darkfall, I return to claim.
Detect
new-trying gritty clicky voice of thousands;
a chord of assembly tuning its domestic.
(Note, each colony different,
an amicable pitch inside all else.)

I listen
to the insular, poached wild body under the bonnet.

Finder, keeper. Life's instrument.

This in my arms (this heavy box) I take to the apiary.
I look at the road we have to cross.
You are not fully ordinary, bees.
The ordinary mortals go by in cars.

ACKNOWLEDGEMENTS

Acknowledgements are due to the editors of *Blaze Vox*, *Granta*, *London Review of Books*, *Poetry Ireland Review*, *Poetry Review*, *The Rialto*, and the organisers of the Bridport Prize. A few bee poems appeared as a pamphlet, *Pages from Bee Journal* (Isinglass).

Grateful thanks to Chris Lewis-Smith who keeps the bees with me, Alan Weaver for explaining over the telephone how to catch a swarm, and Julian Willford for supplying our first colony.

I am indebted to Jane Borodale, Derek Southall, Jon Hill, Valerie Hill, Annie Hunt, Sam Hunt, David Beatty, Kitty Aldridge, Robin Robertson, Peter Straus and Carol Ann Duffy.

THE HISTORY OF VINTAGE

The famous American publisher Alfred A. Knopf (1892–1984) founded Vintage Books in the United States in 1954 as a paperback home for the authors published by his company. Vintage was launched in the United Kingdom in 1990 and works independently from the American imprint although both are part of the international publishing group, Random House.

Vintage in the United Kingdom was initially created to publish paperback editions of books bought by the prestigious literary hardback imprints in the Random House Group such as Jonathan Cape, Chatto & Windus, Hutchinson and later William Heinemann, Secker & Warburg and The Harvill Press. There are many Booker and Nobel Prize-winning authors on the Vintage list and the imprint publishes a huge variety of fiction and non-fiction. Over the years Vintage has expanded and the list now includes great authors of the past – who are published under the Vintage Classics imprint – as well as many of the most influential authors of the present. In 2012 Vintage Children's Classics was launched to include the much-loved authors of our youth.

For a full list of the books Vintage publishes,
please visit our website
www.vintage-books.co.uk

For book details and other information about the classic authors we publish, please visit the Vintage Classics website
www.vintage-classics.info

www.vintage-classics.info